FOR

MOM

HAPPY MOTHER'S
DAY 2002!

D0187905

101 Reasons Why You're the Greatest Mom

By Virginia Reynolds

Illustrated by Mary Kay Krell

Peter Pauper Press, Inc
WHITE PLAINS, NEW YORK

For Trudy, my Florida mom

Designed by Arlene Greco

Illustrations by Mary Kay Krell
copyright © 2000 and licensed by
Art Licensing Properties, L.L.C.,
Reproduced by Bentley House®

Text copyright © 2000
Peter Pauper Press, Inc.
202 Mamaroneck Avenue
White Plains, NY 10601
All rights reserved
ISBN 0-88088-514-9
Printed in China
7 6 5 4 3 2 1

101 Reasons Why You're the Greatest Mom

— 1 —

You can spell "love"
a thousand different ways.

– 2 –

You taught me that
sometimes it's OK to color
outside the lines.

– 3 –

You paved the road for me,
but let me make
my own journey.

– 4 –

You encourage me
to go as far as my dreams
will take me.

– 5 –

You may let me out
of your sight, but never
out of your heart.

- 6 -

You always go to bat for me
when things get tough.

- 7 -

You know that "home"
isn't a place—it's a state
of mind.

~ 8 ~

You scared away the
monsters under the bed.

~ 9 ~

You know exactly when
to be nurse, teacher,
cheerleader, friend.

— 10 —

You showed me the
difference between
stark honesty and
compassionate diplomacy.

—11—

Your enthusiasm
is contagious!

– 12 –

You taught me to accept
life's little setbacks with
style and grace.

-13-

You were never too tired
to read me a story.

-14-

You understand that
chocolate is one of the
major food groups.

– 15 –

You demonstrate with
all your gestures that
"love is in the details."

– 16 –

You remember that
life's too short to
hold grudges.

– 17 –

You still make sure that
I eat my vegetables, and
get to bed at a decent hour.

– 18 –

You'd feed the world if
you could, and send
everyone home
with leftovers.

– 19 –

You taught me never to
settle for second best.

– 20 –

You're the president
(for life) of my fan club.

– 21 –

You turned the refrigerator
door into a priceless
art gallery filled with
my masterpieces.

– 22 –

You were never afraid
to let me get dirty.

– 23 –

You keep moving the goal
posts—so I can achieve more
than I thought I could.

– 24 –

You can see both sides of
every question.

– 25 –

You're the only one who could
fluff the pillows just right
when I was sick.

– 26 –

You made holidays magical,
and turned ordinary days
into holidays.

– 27 –

You taught me all the
important stuff—
like how to spot a
great bargain.

– 28 –

You didn't give me
everything I wanted,
but you always gave me
what I needed.

-29-

You can find a nice word to
say about everybody.

-30-

You really know
how to brag!

— 31 —

You helped me develop
my natural talents.

— 32 —

You can turn a simple meal
into a work of art.

~33~

You taught me to appreciate the occasional dandelion in the lawn of life.

– 34 –

You showed me the Big Picture
(and I don't mean TV!)

– 35 –

You praise all my
achievements, no matter
how small.

~ 36 ~

You're cool—my friends
think so, too.

~ 37 ~

You may get angry, but
it's usually a brief
storm before the sun
comes out again.

– 38 –

You taught me
that the quiet times also
have their place.

~ 39 ~

You gave me just
enough freedom.

~ 40 ~

You're my port in rough seas;
you're my rudder when
I'm drifting.

– 41 –

You taught me
to look before I leap—
but sometimes,
to just close my
eyes and jump.

~ 42 ~

You know all my
faults—and you love me
just the same.

~ 43 ~

You never outgrew
being a kid yourself.

- 44 -

You showed me how
to admit I'm wrong—
gracefully.

- 45 -

You encouraged me
to wear sensible shoes
(sometimes).

– 46 –

You filled our home
with love and laughter.

– 47 –

You taught me that
"money doesn't grow
on trees."

~ 48 ~

You know the value
of all the little things.

– 49 –

Your restaurant was
always "open"
(well, almost always).

– 50 –

You let me make a mess—
and showed me how to
clean it up myself.

— 51 —

You never say,
"I told you so"
(OK, well, maybe
once in a while).

~ 52 ~

You don't mind

getting a

little silly sometimes.

— 53 —

Your cookbook is filled
with recipes for caring,
warmth and compassion.

– 54 –

You wear so many hats—
mom, wife, neighbor,
friend—and you wear
them so stylishly!

– 55 –

You never play favorites.

– 56 –

You set high standards
for me, and showed me
how to set them
for myself.

– 57 –

You know I'm never
too old for hugs, milk,
and cookies.

– 58 –

You've really learned a lot
since I was a kid!

~ 59 ~

You made the hard lessons
easier to bear with soft words
and loving arms.

– 60 –

You can make even a rainy
day sparkle with the sunshine
of your smile.

– 61 –

You know what's important: a
scraped knee, a butterfly, a
school project.

- 62 -

You know I'm not perfect,
but you don't keep
reminding me.

- 63 -

You may be my mom,
but you're your
own woman.

– **64** –

You taught me that nothing's
impossible if you believe
in yourself.

– **65** –

You're able to pause, take a
deep breath, and admire the
beauty of a sunset.

– 66 –

You can strike the spark
that sets off fireworks in
my imagination.

– 67 –

You worried about me a lot
when I was growing up, but
you didn't let it hold me back.

– 68 –

You can whip up 50 cupcakes
for the class picnic faster
than anyone on earth.

- 69 -

You weren't afraid to make
an unpopular decision if it
was for my own good.

– 70 –

You could go out every day
and save the world, and still
find time to make dinner.

– 71 –

Your love spreads out like the
branches of a tree, sheltering
what grows beneath.

- 72 -

You see genius in
my ideas—even the
wildest ones!

- 73 -

You taught me how to
move life's mountains one
stone at a time.

-74-

You give me the courage
of a lion when I'm feeling
like a mouse.

- 75 -

Your values are an anchor
to steady me in the
roughest weather.

- 76 -

You know it's OK to
yield to temptation
once in awhile.

- 77 -

Your love flows like a
stream—fast and sure,
still and peaceful, always
life-giving.

- 78 -

You taught me never to dwell
on my mistakes, but to learn
from them and move on.

~ 79 ~

You live every day
to the fullest.

~ 80 ~

You've given me a lifetime
of warm memories . . .
with more to come!

– 81 –

Your hands are sculpting
a "masterpiece-in-
progress" : me!

– 82 –

You know that, like fine
wine, some things require
time and patience.

– 83 –

You see a misunderstood
flower where other people
see a weed.

– 84 –

You made every outing into
an exciting adventure.

– 85 –

You are the loom that
weaves the tapestry
of our family.

– 86 –

You love me for who I am,
and who I am becoming.

~ 87 ~

You skip around obstacles
without missing a beat.

- 88 -

You make it look

so easy.

- 89 -

You always come

through in a pinch.

- 90 -

Your sweet exterior conceals
steely strength.

- 91 -

You know how to use
laughter as a healing balm.

– 92 –

You really do have eyes
in the back of your head
(you do, don't you?).

– 93 –

You taught me to follow my
heart when everybody else
was following the herd.

- 94 -

You may disagree with
what I say, but you'll defend
my right to say it.

- 95 -

You have the ability to look
at the world through
somebody else's eyes.

- 96 -

You showed me where
to find the silver lining
in every cloud.

– 97 –

You're always holding my
hand, even if you're a
thousand miles away.

– 98 –

You're there for me when
the chips are down . . . and
you make them seem like
chocolate chips!

- 99 -

You promised that I would thank you some day—and you were right!

– 100 –

You can be imitated,
but you can never be
duplicated!

– 101 –

You made me proud
to be who I am—
your child!